Cat and Dog Go Shopping

Cat and Dog went to the shirt store.
They looked at small, medium, and large shirts.

"I need a small," said Dog.
"I need a small, too," said Cat.

Cat and Dog went to get pizza.
They looked at small, medium, and large pizzas.

"I'll have a small pizza," said Dog.
"I'll have a large pizza," said Cat.

Cat and Dog went to the movies.
They looked at small, medium, and large popcorn.

"I'll have a small popcorn," said Dog.
"I'll have a large popcorn," said Cat.

Cat and Dog went to the shirt store.
They looked at small, medium, and large shirts.

"I need a small," said Dog.
"I need a medium," said Cat.

Cat and Dog went to a restaurant.
They looked at small, medium, and large sodas.

"I'll have a small soda," said Dog.
"I'll have a large soda," said Cat.

Cat and Dog went to the ice-cream store.
They looked at small, medium,
and large ice-cream cones.

"I'll have a small ice-cream cone," said Dog.
"I'll have a large ice-cream cone," said Cat.

Cat and Dog went to the shirt store.
They looked at small, medium, and large shirts.

"I need a small," said Dog.
"I need a large," said Cat.

Cat and Dog went to get hamburgers.
"I'll have a small hamburger," said Dog.
"I'll have a small hamburger, too," said Cat.